I0168911

Margaret Stokes

Notes on the Cross of Cong

Margaret Stokes

Notes on the Cross of Cong

ISBN/EAN: 9783337337209

Printed in Europe, USA, Canada, Australia, Japan

Cover: Foto ©Lupo / pixelio.de

More available books at **www.hansebooks.com**

NOTES

ON THE

CROSS OF CONG

.

BY

MARGARET STOKES

HONORARY MEMBER

OF

THE ROYAL IRISH ACADEMY, AND OF THE ROYAL SOCIETY OF ANTIQUARIES OF IRELAND

Printed at the Dublin University Press

BY PONSONBY AND WELDRICK

FOR PRIVATE CIRCULATION ONLY

1895

THE CROSS OF CONG.

LOSE on fifty-six years ago Professor MacCullagh presented and described to the Academy the beautiful reliquary of the True Cross which we term the Cross of Cong. Originally made for the Church of Tuam, it was relegated to the use of the Augustinian Abbots of Cong, where it was preserved till the final extinction of the Order, as connected with that Abbey, in the last century.

The memory of the eminent man to whose generosity we owe the possession of this inestimable treasure will live throughout all time in the history of his country. Although it may be said that his fame rests chiefly on his original researches in Mathematical and Physical Science, yet the services for which the Academy owes to Professor MacCullagh a debt of lasting gratitude are not confined to his scientific labours and discoveries. The nature of his mind was so large that he could duly measure the value and importance of such works of antique art as this reliquary, and enter into the labours of those whose special studies were in the fields of Archæology and Art. Among such friends he numbered George Petrie, who, in words of deep affection and respect, has placed upon record the facts of this gift to the Museum.

Seventeen years before its presentation, Petrie saw this cross for the first time, when, on the occasion of his tour in Connaught, he visited the last mitred Abbot of Cong, then living in retirement in a

B

little cottage at Abbotstown, and who had found the reliquary in a chest
of oak kept in a cottage in the town, where it had lain concealed
probably since the Reformation, or at least subsequent to the rebellion
of 1641. When some time afterwards Petrie communicated his opinion
as to its great historical interest and value to Professor MacCullagh, the
latter, without having ever seen it himself, or having received any further
information relative to it than that which Petrie conveyed to him, purchased it at his own sole expense. On the 24th June, 1839, he presented
it to the Museum of the Royal Irish Academy, which then consisted
mainly of the Underwood Collection, purchased in 1837, and the Collection of Stone Implements given by the King of Denmark. In presenting
this cross, Professor MacCullagh stated that his motive for doing so
was, that by putting it in the possession of a public body, he would
secure it from that shameful process of destruction to which everything
venerable in Ireland had been exposed for centuries, and would contribute
to the formation of our National Collection. By this act he crowned
the efforts of those who, for ten years before, had been labouring to
form our great Museum.

The history of this reliquary is based upon the information afforded
by the five inscriptions which fill the silver edges of the cross, and
which, besides giving the names of the king for whom it was made
and of contemporary dignitaries of the Church, preserve that of the
artist himself, Maelísu MacBratdan O'Echan :—

> In this cross is preserved the cross on which the founder of the
> world suffered.
>
> Pray for Mureduch U Dubthaig, the Senior of Erin.
>
> Pray for Therdel[buch] U Choncho[bair], for the king of Erin, for
> whom this shrine was made.
>
> Pray for Domnall Mac Flannacan U Dub[thaig], bishop of Connacht
> and comarb of Chomman and Ciaran, under whose superinten-
> dence the shrine was made.
>
> Pray for Maelísu Mac Bratdan U Echan, who made this shrine.

I offer here a facsimile drawing of these inscriptions, made by me in the year 1860.

+ HAC CRUCE CRUX : TEGITUR QUÁ PASUS CONDITOR ORBIS
ÓR DO MUREDUCH U IDUBTHAIC DO SENOIR EREND
ÓR DO THEREDÉL U CHONCHÓ DC RÍG EREND LAS-AN-DERBNAD IN CRESSA
ÓR DO DOMNULL MC FLANNACAN U DUBD ERSRUP CONNACHT DO CHOMARBA CHOMMAN ACUS CHIA-
RÁN ICAN ERRNAD IN CRESSA ÓR DO MAELÍSU MC BRATDAN U ECHAN DO RIGHI IN CRESSA

Dr. Petrie has made the following remarks upon these inscriptions in a paper read before the Royal Irish Academy, May, 1850, Proc. Royal Irish Academy, Vol. IV., p. 572 :—

'This series of inscriptions, the first of which is in Latin, and in the old letter, runs all along the edge of the cross, telling its history, and that its purpose was to enshrine a portion of the true cross.

' ✠ HAC CRUCE CRUX TEGITUR QUA PAS[S]US CONDITOR ORBIS.

'Of the different persons whose names are recorded, with the exception of the artist or maker, of whom no other account has been found, many historical notices are preserved in our authentic annals; and one of these authorities also records the bringing of the piece of the true cross into Ireland, and the making of this shrine for its

preservation.   It occurs in the Annals of Inisfallen, at the year 1123,
the year in which the first General Council of Lateran was held,
during the pontificate of Pope Calixtus, and is to the following
effect :—

    ' "A bit of the true cross came into Ireland, and was enshrined
at Roscommon by Turlough O'Conor."

    'This entry in our annals gives us all the information that is pre-
served to us in reference to this relic, which was probably the first of
the kind that was sent to Ireland, although we are told by O'Halloran
of an earlier gift of a piece of the holy cross, by Pope Pascal II., to
Murtogh, the grandson of Brian Boroimhe, and Monarch of Ireland
"with opposition," in the year 1110; and that in honour of this piece
of the cross, the Abbey of Holy Cross, in Tipperary, was founded about
sixty years afterwards.   But, as O'Halloran gives us no authority for
this statement, and though a piece of the cross was preserved there,
and still exists, it is more probable that it was not sent into Ireland
till the time of the erection of that monastery, which was in 1169.'

    The remaining inscriptions are in Irish, and give the names of
the four persons under whose superintendence this shrine for the holy
relic was made.   The first was Muireadach O'Duffy, Archbishop of
Connaught, for whose use it was intended ; the second was the King
Turlough O'Conor, at whose desire and expense it was executed ; the
third, Donnel O'Duffy, was the bishop who watched over its progress ;
and the fourth, Maelisu O'Echan, was the artist who executed it.   Of
the last mentioned, and now most interesting of those four men, no
other record can be found ; no monument is left to tell of his former
greatness save the exquisite work that has stood for more than seven
hundred years, bearing witness to the marvellous power and delicate
skill of the artist.

Muireadach O'Duffy, the senior or archbishop, for whose use this cross was made, was a very illustrious man, whose death is thus recorded in 'The Annals of the Four Masters':—

'A.D. 1150, Muireadach O'Duffy, Archbishop of Connaught, the arch-senior of Ireland in wisdom, in chastity, in the bestowal of gifts and food, died at Cong, on the 16th day of May, on the festival of St. Brendan, in the seventy-fifth year of his age.'

King Turlough O'Conor, under whose care and at whose desire the work was wrought, was surnamed the Augustus of Western Europe. He reigned fifty years in Ireland, and raised the power of Connaught higher than it ever was before. He was magnificent and generous in many of his acts, and zealously cultivated the arts of civilized life, as we learn from such existing remains as the richly-adorned church and cross of Tuam, as well as the work now in question.

The bishop, Donnel O'Duffy, who is described as the ecclesiastic under whose superintendence the shrine was made, was also distinguished in his time, and this family of O'Duffy in Connaught appears to have been peculiarly devoted to religion. Five instances of members of it may be enumerated who were abbots, bishops, or archbishops, and the market cross at Cong was erected by two of this name who were abbots of that place.

Having the information thus afforded by the inscriptions on this reliquary, we confidently repeat the words of Professor Mac Cullagh when he speaks of it as 'a most interesting memorial of the period preceding the English invasion, and one which shows a very high state of art in the country at the time when it was made.'

We may now proceed to describe the reliquary itself whose delicate proportions make it an object of extreme grace and loveliness. The shaft of this cross measures two feet six inches high; its breadth or span of arms, one foot six and three-quarter inches; thickness of shaft and arms, one and three-quarter inches. It is formed of oak, covered with

plates of copper outside, which are placed five on the front and three
on the back, with a portion of a fourth plate of brass.   These are
divided into thirty-eight compartments down the face of the cross, which
are filled in with fine interlaced filigree gold work fastened by rivets to
the plates beneath.   Thirteen stones or enamels remain of the eighteen

THE CROSS OF CONG (REVERSE SIDE).

which were disposed at regular intervals along the edges, and on the
face of the shaft and arms, and spaces remain for nine others which
were placed at intervals down the centre.   Two beads of blue and white

enamel remain out of the four settings which surrounded the central
boss. The shaft terminates below in the grotesque head of an animal,
beneath which it is attached to a spherical elaborately ornamented ball,
surmounting the socket in which was inserted the pole or shaft for
carrying the cross.

The back of the cross is decorated with bosses of crimson enamel
and is divided into four panels, containing golden interlaced work of
a larger character than that on the front, but showing great freedom and
grace of design. The strap or cord, by which the two pieces of wood
within were originally tied crosswise, seems to have been represented by
two bands of bronze; the hollowed spaces into which they fitted at the
junction of the shaft and arms of the cross are still remaining.

Professor Mac Cullagh adds: ' In the centre of the arms, at their
junction with the shaft, there is fixed a cruciform piece of oak, marked
with the figure of a cross, and much older apparently than the rest of
the wood, which is oak also. This piece bears marks of the knife, as if
it had been taken for the relic; though it is perhaps too large to be so,
and, besides, it does not appear that the true cross was made of oak.
Hereabouts, however, the relic certainly was; for the place is sur-
mounted by a very conspicuous crystal of quartz—a mode of exhibiting
such things that seems to be alluded to by Chaucer in the Canterbury
Tales, where he makes his " Pardoner" say—

> ' " Then show I forth my longé crystal stonés,
> Ycramméd full of cloutés and of bonés ;
> Relics they be, as weenen they each one."

' The shape of the crystal is remarkable. Thin lenses, such as we
have now, were not invented in those days, nor for a long time after ;
and the present specimen of a thick one, which could be of no use
in viewing an object, unless placed in immediate contact with it, is to
be classed among the lenticular gems of quartz or rock-crystal, which
Dr. Priestley says "are supposed to have belonged to the Druids."'

The objection raised by Professor MacCullagh in this passage, as to the material of the small cruciform piece of wood inserted in this reliquary, is met by the fact that this is not the only instance on record in which such relics appear to be of oak. The relic of the Holy Wood in the College of St. Gregory at Downside, near Bath, is described by Rohault de Fleury as resembling old oak:

'Les veines sont larges, la surface est luisante et présente l'apparence d'une grande dureté. La couleur est noirâtre ou plutôt d'un riche brun; le bois dont il semble se rapprocher davantage est *le vieux chêne*, mais sans les marques transversales qu'on voit dans le chêne.'

Again, he says at page 61:

'Juste Lipse veut qu'elle soit d'un seul bois et *en chêne*, parce que des hommes dignes de foi l'attestent, que cet arbre est commun en Judée, que son bois est solide et propre à cet usage.'

He also mentions that the famous Anglo-Saxon reliquary of the true cross now in Brussels, belonging to the Church of SS. Gudule and Michael, contains a fragment of the Holy Wood, described as the largest known, which is of the colour of old oak, the veining being scarcely visible. Yet the result of a very close examination is to make it appear to be a resinous wood.

In the great work of Rohault de Fleury, entitled 'Mémoires sur les Instruments de la Passion,' from which these remarks are taken, he devotes the first book to the history of the holy wood of the cross on which the Saviour died, and the dispersion of its fragments throughout Europe and the East, Ireland being the only country omitted from the list of places thus signalised, although her annals bear witness to the fact that on two occasions, in the twelfth century, such relics were sent here; and it may be questioned whether any shrine for such exists elsewhere as beautiful as is this Cross of Cong.

We learn that in the end of the eighth century Charlemagne gave to the church of Aix-la-Chapelle a portion of the true cross, which was enshrined in a small cross worn by him. This was a pectoral cross, not belonging to the same class as ours, and it has long since disappeared.

Between the years 871 and 901 it is stated by tradition that a fragment of the true cross was given to King Alfred, and afterwards belonged to Glastonbury; but its present shrine only dates from the time of Charles I.

About the year 1028, Robert Duke of Normandy obtained a piece of the true cross from his tutor, Arnulph: this was also enshrined in a pectoral cross.

About the year 1050, Queen Margaret of Croatia gave to the church of St. Stephen, at Ragusa, two pieces of the true cross, which were then enshrined in a cross of silver. This reliquary, as I learn from Mr. Arthur Evans, no longer exists. In 1667 the church of St. Stephen at Ragusa, together with the cathedral founded by Cœur-de-Lion, was destroyed by a great earthquake.

In the year 1109, Anselm, a priest in Jerusalem, gave a portion of the true cross to Galon, bishop of Paris. This was enshrined in a cross of engraved crystal, which was fixed in a large cross of silver. The reliquary was preserved at Notre Dame till 1793. But since the sack of the archbishopric in 1828, it has disappeared, and fragments of the wood are shown in separate reliquaries, which are merely of modern workmanship.

The reliquary which may with most profit be compared with the Cross of Cong is the Anglo-Saxon cross in the treasury of the church of SS. Gudule et Michael, at Brussels.* This cross has passed through many more vicissitudes and suffered greater injury than the Irish one, and, unfortunately, it seems impossible to fix its date with perfect accuracy. It is believed by some to have been made to contain a portion of the true cross brought from the Holy Land by Thierry III. in 1039, or Thierry VI. in 1139. It is said to be identical with the reliquary

* Described by H. Logeman. See 'Mémoires couronnés et autres Mémoires publiés par l'Académie Royale de Belgique.' 1891. Vol. xlv.

cross presented to Albert and Isabella about the year 1615. In 1793 it was shorn of its precious ornaments by the Sansculottes. When M. H. Logeman examined it in 1890, he discovered an Anglo-Saxon inscription running round the silver plate, with these words—

Drahmal me worhte;

and, running down the sides of the reliquary, there is a quotation from some old version of Caedmon, which may be translated—

> 'The Cross is my name.
> Once I bore the mighty King,
> Trembling bedewed with blood.'

> 'This cross Aethlmer had to make, and Adhel-wold his brother,
> To the glory of Christ, for the soul of Aelfric their brother.'

The object of these remarks is to show the relative position occupied by the Cross of Cong in the history of Christian Art. Out of the six reliquaries of this type which have been discovered, only two still exist—we mean the reliquary, in the form of a cross, made to contain a fragment of the true cross. Fragments of the wood were often preserved in caskets and shrines of other forms, with which we do not deal at present. The two crosses of this type are—The Cross at Brussels and the Cross of Cong. These two may be treated as contemporary, although, judging from what is left of the art of this Anglo-Saxon reliquary, the figures engraved upon it of the Four Evangelists, etc., the authorities in the British Museum are inclined to think it belongs to the close of the eleventh century. We know that the Cross of Cong dates from the beginning of the twelfth, from the year 1123. As all the ornaments which covered the face of the panels in the Anglo-Saxon cross are lost, the result of a comparison between the two reliquaries is less likely to be successful; nevertheless, the little nails or rivets which remain on the face of these plates being perfectly similar to those by which the filigree ornaments that fill the panels of the Cross of Cong are fixed, it is natural to suppose that it also was covered with filigree. Such filigree seems to have been characteristic of early French art, since most of the crosses attributed to St. Eloi were covered with such adornment. We see it on the Cross of Notre-Dame, at Paris, as well as on those attributed to him at Grandmont. It has been held by Abbé Texier that there is nothing characteristic or individual in this work by which we could assign a place or period to an object thus adorned. This does not apply to the arts of these islands; for while in France the threads are seen to run in light and graceful foliate scrolls upon their foundation of silver-gilt plates, or to twirl in volutes and circles which form bosses, the designs in Ireland are bolder, and generally interlaced zoo-morphic patterns.

Nevertheless, the growth of a wider, a less local and archaic taste is manifest in the design of such a work as this cross, as compared with other examples of the goldsmith's art in Ireland. The divergent spirals, so characteristic of all purely Irish work of a previous century, have entirely disappeared. It would seem as if the movement which took place at the end of the eleventh century in France had extended its influence to Ireland. The Crusades gave a great impulse to the goldsmith's art all throughout Europe, creating a demand for shrines in which to preserve the sacred relics brought home by the soldiers of the faith; and Suger, Abbot of St. Denis, gave additional impetus to the consecration of art to the service of religion. This advance continued till the thirteenth century, which may be considered the very zenith of ecclesiastical art. The artist who wrought the chalice bearing the name of Suger, which was stolen in 1804; or he who made the corona of Aix-la-Chapelle; or the shrine in which Frederic I. collected the bones of Charlemagne, in the Louvre; or the gold-mounted vase of Queen Eleonora, in the Cluny Museum; or the candelabra in the Imperial Library of Paris; or the so-called chalice of St. Remy, now at Rheims, were the contemporaries of Maelísu O'Echan while he was at work in Roscommon enshrining this fragment of the holy cross. It is by comparison with these works that we can learn what were the correspon-

dencies and what the idiosyncracies of Irish art. And we may be sure
the same education was expected of the Irish as of the French goldsmith, an idea of which may be formed from the description of the
industrial arts of his time, given, in the days of Suger, by the artist-
monk, Theophilus. He was to prepare and purify his own material; to
cast his own waxen models; to draw with the compass, and portray the
subjects graven on the silver—he was to be at once modeller, sculptor,
smelter, enameller, jewel-mounter, and inlay-worker. And at the close
of his exordium Theophilus adds these words :—

    ' Act therefore now, well-intentioned man, happy before God and
men in this life, happier in a future, in whose labour and study so
many sacrifices are offered up to God; henceforth warm thyself with
more ample invention, hasten to complete with all the study of thy
mind those things which are still needed in the House of the Lord.'

www.ingramcontent.com/pod-product-compliance
Lightning Source LLC
Chambersburg PA
CBHW031159090426
42738CB00008B/1397